How Academics Get Published

PUBLISHED

DEMYSTIFYING

Book Publishers' Expectations

OF ACADEMIC AUTHORS

How Academics Get Published

First Published in 2024 by Lightbooks,
an imprint of Lentswe La Lesedi (Pty) Ltd

PO Box 2365, Gaborone, Botswana

lightbooksbotswana@gmail.com
publisher@lightbooks.co.bw

www.charlesbewlay.com

ISBN: 978-99912-71-69-9 (Print – black)

Cover Design: Charles Bewlay
Cover artwork: Olga Turner
Typesetting, Layout and Design: Lentswe La Lesedi
Book and form illustrations: Lentswe La Lesedi

You know that I write slowly. This is chiefly because I am never satisfied until I have said as much as possible in a few words, and writing briefly takes far more time than writing at length.
Carl Friedrich Gauss

Times are bad. Children no longer obey their parents, and everyone is writing a book.
Marcus Tullius Cicero

Nullius in verba.[1]
Motto of the Royal Society

---

[1] Literally 'On the word of no one', or more idiomatically translated as, 'Take nobody's word for it'. Every academic's motto. Evidence.

Writing this small book has given me more admiration for all the authors with whom I have made friendships, and gained great respect for, over many decades. We have travelled together in these most rewarding of lives, writing and publishing.

Contents

PREFACE

Originally an ebook, this monograph has transitioned into paperback format, which many prefer. Here are a few notes on navigating your way through it.

The book has two types of asides, *Tips* and *Anecdotes*. The *Tips*, highlighted with a border, offer specific additional practical guidance. The *Anecdotes*, with a grey highlight, share stories from the writer's experiences, and I trust will sometimes amuse you – publishing can be, and often is, fun.

There are many clickable links in the ebook to direct you to specific websites or sections within it to make your life a bit easier. The external links in the ebook are footnotes here in the print edition.

Also in this print edition is an index, which is not available in the ebook due to to the reflowable text nature of ebooks.

******

For a nominal price, you can purchase the companion ebook, which you can find at

https://books2read.com/u/3kDZDK, or

https://www.amazon.co.uk/dp/B0CPG15FN4, or

preferably direct from me at

https://charlesbewlay.gumroad.com/l/ddtnb

******

All the illustrations from books and forms are generously provided by my publisher. Any further illustrations may be from free unaccredited sources, and every effort has been made to contact the copyright owners. Should I be contacted by such, I would be happy to pay any reasonable permission fees.

Chapter 1.
PRELUDE

Welcome to my publishing world. Here I'll be showing you how to avoid the blunders and hurdles in your rock-strewn path of getting your academic work published, as a book, *by a publisher* and not a vanity publisher (see Chapter 3). I will show you what good publishers expect along the way. I want you to get published. My aim is to demystify the whole process.

As a seasoned book publisher, I want to share decades of experience with you. From the frontlines of editing and proofreading to commissioning, designing, and laying out books, as well as marketing and project managing, I have been deeply involved in every aspect of book production throughout my career. While working for a highly regarded multinational publisher during my first ten years, I gained the beginnings of my skills and knowledge. Then in my niche publishing company, I took on everything, learning continuously, investigating the depths, taking on new directions, sometimes stumbling and falling, but never drowning. Now, here is my 'inside story' of what I've learnt; *for you*.

There are a few classic and brilliant works relating to what I have to say here, but I did find them somewhat lengthy and costly, some even outdated. And without a doubt, you're busy. So you probably want to make the best use of your time, possibly your most valuable asset, and I thought you would prefer distilled wisdom to the whole library.

I have set out to provide you with a solid overview of how to get your book published, and how to navigate the publishing process. Additionally, I have notes on ways in which you can contribute to sales and marketing. What I write is based on my experience, but does draw on the wisdom of others, gained over the years. I include references for additional reading at the end of the text, as well as in the footnotes.

I also give some detail and resources for those who wish to take up the self-publishing route. A large part of what I write is just as true for a self-published book: the processes hardly diverge.

Chapter 2.
Symbiosis: the core of publishing

To a large extent, this monograph is about a symbiosis of three *core* partners who are part of producing a book: the writer, the publisher and the reader. These are three independent entities who choose to enter a mutual dependency, a symbiotic relationship. Each of the three partners becomes dependent on the other, for:

✓ without the writer there is nothing;

✓ without readers' needs and wants, a book will simply not have any readers;

✓ without the publisher, the writer's words may not be ever seen by many readers in the most viable, attractive and readable form possible, as a book. The publisher 'makes it happen' through a complex and holistic process.

Many roles are involved in making a book 'happen' holistically, within a publisher's domain of this symbiosis. There are editors, artists, readers, typesetters and designers, as well as promotion, sales, marketing, publicity and advertising staff, warehouse people, stock controllers, drivers, and key ancillary and administrative staff. Many of these may be freelancers, and many jobs are combined in smaller companies. And, we must not forget the managers, financiers, bookkeepers and accountants: to them falls the question of providing risk information and royalty calculations, among much else. But it is the human 'publisher' who pulls all these people together, and who makes the decisions to publish, or not. The publisher is also responsible for dealings with the other external players, notably the printers and the booksellers, including the online bookstores. In some cases, a literary agent[2] may represent the author and share responsibility with the publisher in such matters as getting reviews. In the age of artificial intelligence (AI), humans still make the publishing investment decisions: it's their money, after all.

It is not my purpose here to detail the whole of a publisher's operation (but I do provide a quick list of stages is in Appendix A). Rather, I want

---

[2] Agents: literary agents are not of our concern here as they do not play a large role in academic publishing.

to highlight one of the publisher's prime roles: getting all the people involved to work together holistically. This is to ensure that the writer's words and wisdom get to the reader in the best form, on time. The printers and the booksellers, ebook makers and web designers, on the street or on the web, also have their own workforces, employing many.

A second key role of the publisher of academic books is manuscript selection. It is often an extremely difficult process to establish the viability of a manuscript and assess how much risk to take. There exists no formula, no guidebook, no bible on this. Publishing constantly faces the difficulties of the marketplace (small or large), distribution, and pricing. Too many or too large risks that go wrong will fold a publisher. See more later on in Chapter 5 on commissioning and acquisitions editors.

Risk: this is what a publisher takes every time an author's manuscript is accepted. Evaluating it is a not easily acquired skill. It is always there, something that needs managing and working on. Also, authors[3] do play a major part in minimising that risk, in their own interest. Also, see later in Chapter 11, 'Sales and marketing'.

I once had a superb salesman who I thought had promise on the marketing side. I even sent him on a short course overseas. Despite my efforts and the course, he never got to grips with forecasting sales, so that I could assess potential publications' risks. He went on to a great sales manager and PR chap.

An interesting take on risk is in the use of open access (OA). Here the cost of online books, monographs or journal articles is paid for by the author's research funders or institution. This book processing charge (or article processing charge in the case of journals or book chapters) reduces a publisher's risk, although peer reviews can be done at a cost to the publisher, who will have to recoup this. OA is dealt with in more detail in Chapter 9, under 'Open Access' on page 36.

---

[3] This chapter also applies in greater part to editors of multi-author works and conference proceedings. It is their job to cajole and encourage the writers, but they may well end up having to do some of the work themselves. See the section on page 43 in Chapter 10 on this.

Chapter 3.
GETTING PUBLISHED VS. SELF-PUBLISHING

Getting published

As an academic, a scholar, you will need to publish with a publisher recognised by your institution and peers in your discipline, not by a vanity publisher (see below). If, that is, you want your publication to count towards your reputation, résumé and promotion prospects. The reason for this is the scrutiny that a good publisher will undertake to decide assess the quality of the manuscript, and whether to risk publication. The same scrutiny applies to OA publications, which I shall also discuss in the dedicated section in Chapter 9, 'Open Access'. The author may also seek to find a subsidy independently, and the cost may be included in a research grant or scholarship. A publisher may help with this.

This is different from self-publishing, which I also discuss below. It should be noted that self-published books have no credibility in the academic world, where peer review and editorial input are regarded as essential.

Self-publishing

This is really beyond the main scope of this book, but I have had requests to include some guidance, so here it is. But, yet again, bear in mind that a self-published academic book may have no credibility among peers. Self-publishers take on the risk themselves. They too can get a subsidy, funding from an external source, either through direct subsidy or by advertising. Crowdfunding is also a possibility (also see more below). Do be aware that there are dozens of self-publishing sites in many countries. Some of them will charge very high fees, and some are scams

I have found that the websites below will give plenty of good advice. They'll all try to hard sell their services, but have tons of help for free.

✓ How Much Does It Cost to Self-Publish a Book in 2023?[4] The site title speaks for itself.

✓ https://selfpublishing.com/ also speaks for itself.

✓ Kindlepreneur at https://kindlepreneur.com/ is aimed at using Ama-

---

[4] https://blog.reedsy.com/guide/how-to-self-publish-a-book/cost-to-self-publish/#-calculator.

zon Kindle formatting and marketing, but has much more.

✓ https://selfpublishingwithdale.com/index.php/resources-for-self-publishers/ also has many resources.

Good self-publishing sites will offer the author many options, from editorial through to marketing, whereas the vanity publisher gives little or no choice. They will also rave on about about how great a manuscript you have, of course! For more see this excellent blog: Book Publishers to Avoid (and Other Shady Author Scams).[5]

Vanity publishing and camera-ready copy outfits

Some self-publishing companies fall into the category of 'vanity publishing', those who have no interest in promoting or selling your book. I have talked to a few authors who have come to me – after they've handed over their cash – and want to know why they didn't get what was expected. Proof corrections are not attended to, queries raised by email are ignored, paid for layout and editing are terrible, and on and on. These vanity publishers will give you a 'unique ISBN' (all ISBNs are unique) and perhaps a few printed copies for you to sell, but everything else you pay for. You must get all the editing, typesetting, proof checking, design and layout done at your cost and time. I have been shown work by a vanity publisher who included terrible editorial and layout in the price, all payable up front. Some vanity publishers even insist on receiving print-ready manuscript, also known as 'camera-ready copy'.[6] The author provides this and the vanity publisher has little or no editorial or design input.

The vanity publisher is a concern, and I do advise you to avoid them at all costs. Some further great advice in this short video There Are Book Publishers To Avoid And New Author Scams.[7]

Assisted self-publishing and hybrid publishing

These are literally a hybrid of traditional risk publishing and self-publishing. The author has higher control, but at the cost of some payments. Higher royalties are often payable as a result. They offer editorial and

---

[5]   https://blog.reedsy.com/guide/publishing-companies-to-avoid/

[6]   Camera-ready means ready to print, and comes from the now rather dated method, but still used, of making film from a printout in order to make printing plates.

[7]   https://justpublishingadvice.com/publishing-companies-to-avoid-and-nasty-new-author-scams/#Writers_beware_Author_Solutions_has_a_reputation

design and layout services. The video How to Avoid Vanity Presses & Author Scams, mentioned above also covers these.[8] There are reputable companies, but the vanity publishers are also edging in, using 'assisted self-publishing' and 'hybrid publishing' in their descriptions.

An excellent read and resource is at IBPA Hybrid Publisher Criteria,[9] also downloadable for reference. Anyhow, as always, *caveat emptor,* let the buyer beware.

The other end of the spectrum: crowdfunding for books

Yes, you may be able to persuade a group of people to help you write and publish your book. Be prepared to put in the serious legwork though, probably months. Two worthwhile sites, both of which list the same crowdfunding sources, are Crowdfunding for Authors: A Simple Guide for 2023[10] and Best Crowdfunding Platforms for Authors to Publish Books.[11] Two further sources on crowdfunding for authors are: Publish Your Knowledge: The Complete Guide to Crowdfunding a Nonfiction Book…,[12] and Kickstarter For Authors With Monica Leonelle[13] (a podcast with a transcript).

Of interest to academics will be Crowdfunding in Higher Education Institutions. Theory and Best Practices,[14] where there's a free pdf outline.

> **Tip:** Self-publishers may want to go on the ebook route. See more on this in the next chapter

---

[8]   https://www.youtube.com/watch?v=IC90ororbXI

[9]   https://www.ibpa-online.org/page/hybrid-publisher-criteria-download

[10] https://selfpublishing.com/crowdfunding-for-authors/

[11] https://www.thebalancemoney.com/best-crowdfunding-platforms-for-authors-985177#citation-14

[12] https://www.goodreads.com/book/show/56247676-publish-your-knowledge

[13] https://www.thecreativepenn.com/2022/03/28/kickstarter-for-authors/

[14] https://www.researchgate.net/publication/372960609_Crowdfunding_in_Higher_Education_ Institutions_Theory_and_Best_Practices

Chapter 4.
ELECTRONIC BOOKS, EBOOKS

Ebooks,[15] are an increasing part of the academic market.[16] The author should expect the same processes to be followed as for printed books.

A major concern of authors and publishers is illegal copying and distribution, piracy. This has led to the particular success of Amazon Kindle and Apple Books, using .mobi and .epub formats respectively, which are impossible to pirate (unless someone's account has been hacked). Other platforms that also provide good secure sales include Barnes and Noble, Kobo, Lulu, Ingram Spark and Smashwords (now under the umbrella of Draft2Digital, a distribution aggregator).

For the self-publisher, creating an ebook is not straightforward. There are many (mostly free) online sites that purport to convert a manuscript in MS Word to ebook format. All of those that I have seen are, frankly, disastrous. But Sigil and Calibre are powerful, free and open source, although complex to use. The leader of the pack has for long been Vellum, but it is only available for the Mac. A recent entry to the fray is Atticus, also available on PCs. Both are pricy. Three other alternatives are Lulu, D2D and Reedsy, all with their limitations.

> **Tip::** A significant difference between printed books and ebooks is in the use of colour: ebooks cost no more to produce in colour than just black and grey. But with printed books, the print costs of colour will be at least double. This can have a major impact on the illustrations you use, with maps particularly.

---

[15] Here's a good example of recent and rapid language evolution: from electronic book > e-Book > eBook or e-book > ebook.

[16] Note that some libraries now only stock newly published books as ebooks.

Chapter 5.
Getting your manuscript accepted: what the publisher looks for

The publisher will assess a manuscript in the four *main* areas below.

✓ Risk: the financial viability, the 'risk-worthiness'

✓ Originality: the main text, the quality and the writing style

✓ The use of language and its editability

✓ Technical aspects: word processor usage and backup.

These will be covered below, with some useful additions under these subheadings – 'The book proposal' and 'Self-editing', 'Notes, foot- and end-,' 'References and citations', 'House style', and 'Textbooks'.

Risk

It is commonly supposed that the 'risk-worthiness' of a manuscript is of no concern to a writer. A writer is, after all, writing from the heart and soul, as well as the mind. A writer's self-belief sustains the effort. But, for the author to be published, he or she should be writing for someone, so needs to be completely cognisant of the target readership. You need to discuss the potential viability of publication early on. This will be with a publisher or their acquisitions editor (sometimes also acquiring editor, and commissioning or publishing editor in the UK).[17] It may save a great deal of heartache later, following suggestions such as 'cut by half' or 're-duce illustrations by fifty per cent' come in; causing all sorts of strong emotions and verbal abuse (mostly internal, of course). That has indeed happened to me, even with a threat to 'beat you up'! See also the next section 'The book proposal'.

The three further areas of manuscript assessment form the main thrust of this chapter. But first we need to look at your starting point, the book proposal, and an important note on self-editing.

Early in my publishing career, there was a history book that I believed was really important – I had even worked many outside work hours on it. (I even wrote a small section on carbon dating since the historian authors

---

[17] I shall use the term 'acquisitions editor' from now on.

couldn't get their heads around this.) I was determined to keep the price below a critical one since I wanted it to be available at a price many could afford. This meant a pretty hefty first print run, and selling the lot in the first year, so my forecasting was also a self-belief that I had to act on. My boss thought I was in dreamland. So I bet my job on it! Mad! This young commissioning editor learnt a great deal about marketing, and kept his job. *Risk!*

The book proposal

Submitting a proposal[18] – sometimes called a proposition – rather than a full manuscript, is generally the best initial step to take with a potential publisher. Although publishers vary, you will probably need to include most of the documents below.

✓ A cover letter, with your name, credentials and address, starting with a request to consider your proposal for publication. Also include an outline of how you are an authority in the field, providing new research or angles on the areas, field or topic(s) you are writing about. Also, indicate at what stage your manuscript is at. And ask if there is interest in seeing your whole manuscript. Give your book a provisional descriptive title that will draw attention and curiosity.

✓ A rationale promoting the qualities of your proposed book, where it fits in the market, potential sales, and how it will better the competition.

✓ A draft outline table of contents. and an indication of what illustrations, tables and charts will be included.

✓ A highly polished sample chapter (or two), at least 1200 words – not the introduction. Remember, you are selling your proposal and your book, so this needs to be a very good chapter, with the best of your writing, showing what you are capable of. Some prefer to use a chapter that they really enjoyed working on, or perhaps a favourite. It must have been fully self-edited (see below).

Before submitting a proposal, make sure that the publisher is a suitable one for your work, has published work of a similar genre, or is perhaps interested in adding something somewhat tangential to their

---

[18] The classic work on proposals is Portwood-Stacer (2021)

'list'. If in doubt, a brief enquiry addressed to an acquisitions editor explaining what you want to publish would be in order.

Remember that your potential publisher and editor are as much after recognition as you are, quite apart from possibly making some money out of it too. They also want you to get good reviews, impress, and even win awards. Remember what I said about symbiosis above?

A publisher may have some capacity to assess a manuscript in house. But, frequently, and always with academic presses, other opinions will be required for peer review. External 'readers' will be briefed to assess the manuscript; more than one reader may be necessary in some circumstances. The publisher will brief the external reader, invariably via a standard questionnaire.

> **Tip::** An academic publisher is primarily looking for originality, for something new, or a new angle on the topic, and of course sales potential. Regurgitation of already existing material rates decidedly low on the publishability scale.

Indeed, the author needs to indicate what makes their book special, and what makes it better than competing works. Non-trivial research is necessary to produce original material of interest to a sufficient number of potential readers.

The author also needs to know how to respond to peer review. There is an excellent article on this at Reader response.[19]

All of the above will equally apply to OA submissions. The same review process will be undertaken.

Also, see Chapter 8 Individual publishers' submission guidelines.

> **Tip:** Most of what follows in this chapter also applies to your sample chapter.

Self-editing

Some authors reckon that editing is only for editors. I have found that this is often true of writers who have been commissioned by an organisation to add a chapter or section to a report. Such writers don't often get asked again. A badly self-edited piece of writing causes many

---

[19] https://manuscriptworks.com/blog/reader-reports

queries to be raised due to lack of clarity, and a lack of enthusiasm on the part of any external editor. Well self-edited writing encourages the external editor to make your writing shimmer, and make you glow. Editors are very human. As soon as you can, meet up with your editor, virtually if in-person isn't viable. A good relationship with your editor is crucial.

Look at your choice of words, spelling, grammar, punctuation, heading levels, illustration and table headings, flow, repetition, citations and references, and that your contents lists are updated. Your indexable words may also need adding or modifying. There are also good tips at 9 Editing Tips,[20] and other sites you can find with a search. Your reputation is on line with every publication your name is in, or on. Additionally, self-editing helps you sharpen your writing skills and brings out the best in your work.

In addition to general self-editing, there are particular areas that need to be carefully looked at for the academic writer. So, to increase the chances of your manuscript or proposal being accepted, what follows is a succinct guide that highlights the most fundamental steps.

Originality: the main text

Your manuscript needs significant *substance*. Arguments must follow clearly and logically. They must be fully substantiated, with evidence for each argument and conclusion. Primary sources need to be drawn on as far as possible, as they lend more weight than secondary ones. The manuscript will receive thorough scrutiny from the publisher, reader, or acquisitions editor, with the term 'justify' being a prevalent consideration in the assessment. It may be hard to believe, but it is actually extremely common to see large numbers of unsubstantiated statements in a manuscript, invariably leading to rejection or severe acceptance delay, due to rewriting. One of the easiest ways of spotting this is the overuse of inappropriate bulleted or numbered lists by 'prescriptive' writers. Sweeping generalisations are made from shreds of evidence, and generalisations that fail to stand any form of test. Readers of books are not interested in simply being told the facts: they want to see them in a rounded, connected and interrelated picture, how they hang together, and how they support a case.

Concise argument is another key matter that will be under consideration. At the far extreme, repetition and yet further unsubstanti-

---

[20] https://blog.reedsy.com/self-editing-tips/#5__replace_adverbs_with_stronger_verbs

ation of argument is unacceptable. The reader is not listening to a sermon in church, and really does not want to be told the same thing time and time again. An argument always needs supporting evidence.

A suitable writing style, which needs to be consistent, and a clear structure are also on the assessment list. All of this should be clear to any author who has been through the rigours of theses presentations. Some authors wrongly seem to forget this, or think that books do not require such rigour. The publisher will also have eyes wide open for plagiarism, looking out for anything that should be contained in citations. The author needs to be extremely careful of using AI in writing. Enough AI text has been shown to be plagiarised to warrant extreme caution, and the author can be liable for copyright infringement. Also see Chapter 6 'Permissions and copyright'.

Prejudged attitudes, including gender bias, racism, neglect of minority interests, and unsubstantiated assertions or allegations are all cause for great concern. Whereas the first three are now generally dealt with well by most authors, and on the decline, there appears to be, regrettably, an increasing number of unsubstantiated allegations in manuscripts that cross my desk. Unfortunately, more and more of this is finding its way into self-published print and ebooks, especially with the growth of vanity publishers.

Notes, foot- and end-

Different publishers have, as do authors, different preferences for whether footnotes or endnotes are preferred, and so do readers. As a general rule, however, footnotes are further justification or need for a better understanding of the text. Endnotes can be referred to, to expand ideas that are not needed for the main thrust of the argument. So both can be used. From a book production point of view, large numbers of footnotes, especially on the same page, may cause difficulty, especially if changes are made to page proofs. Some publishers specify only endnotes (end of chapter or whole text). Additions or deletions to text may, however, leave the footnote on the previous or following page. This will depend on the publisher and the software skills of the designers or typesetter.

From the their point of view, it is easier for a book's reader to bookmark the notes at a book's end rather than bookmarking them at the end of each chapter. The only advantage of endnotes being at the end of each chapter is in multi-contributor books, where an 'offprint' of the author's particular chapter (or journal article) may be needed.

References and citations

These cause more vexation and delay to a publication than any other. This is especially true of multi-author works and conference proceedings. Many a manuscript reader or reviewer has given the thumbs down on the grounds that the references are inadequate. So let's look at some ground rules below, and this necessitates being particularly prescriptive.

- ✓ **All the sources cited** in the text that support arguments must be fully referenced.

- ✓ **The full references list should not contain sources that are not referred to in the text.** These should form a separate list of 'further reading' or 'select bibliography'.

- ✓ **The formats and styles of the references must be consistent**, according to any house style being used, or one prescribed by a publisher. Ask ask your publisher if you have one. And finally...

- ✓ **The references must be complete. Anything cited in the main text** must be presented in full in the references. A source cited in the text that is not in the references should be removed. This, however, can have serious consequences as it may leave a particular argument unsupported. In some cases, the entire argument may fall apart.

Some authors go to the opposite extreme, and feel that they must cite an external source to justify every statement, doing so throughout with foot- or end-notes. The reader, thus confronted, may naturally ask, 'Does this writer have something to say?'. The reader should not be expected to check numerous citations on every page. Over-citation is also an indicator of a poorly constructed argument.

The use of language

There's nothing worse for an editor, reader or reviewer than to be given a manuscript and find it full of typos, spelling mistakes and bad grammar. They'll probably, at best, put it aside till 'later', at worst reject it immediately. Take the time to self-edit your manuscript with a specific focus on language. Bear in mind your readership also. An academic treatise will need a very different approach to that of a textbook.

An acquisitions editor or pre-publication reviewer will want to read the manuscript and get a sense of it quickly. Poorly constructed sentences and weakly structured argument will, in the first place, make any reviewer groan and certainly implant a negative attitude. This alone may lead to a very rapid rejection. Publishers do, however, have a term 'salvageable', meaning that, with a great deal of editorial effort, a manuscript can be salvaged, or made good. But that may not be viable from an economic point of view, so this burden will probably lie with the author. Also see Chapter 9 'Manuscript accepted!' (page 34) on this.

Poor use of language also distracts from the content of a manuscript. The reader can get so bogged down in trying to interpret the language that the sense and logic of the content can be lost.

A few specific and very common language errors and some guidelines on dealing with them can help, as below. Paying attention to them in the self-editing process will improve readability, and any reader's frame of mind, as little can put a reader in a bad mood than seeing continuous language errors. To repeat, these really distract from getting to grips with content.

The innocent comma, surprisingly enough. In general, commas separate ideas in the same way as any punctuation. Your best instant clue to correctness is reading your sentence out loud. The minimalist will avoid commas everywhere, whereas others will sprinkle them like pepper on a plate. Commas should not split an idea. But where there are subclauses in a sentence, the reader should not have to go back to find the meaning. 'The density and the colour of the solvent…' needs no comma, but, 'The density, and this should be measured carefully, and the colour of the solvent…' does. There are two ideas in the latter: if 'The density and this should be measured carefully and the colour of the solvent…' is used, the reader will at least expect another noun after 'and', then will have to re-read to get the sense. The 'pepper-pot' writer will put too many commas in, as in, 'The colour, and density, of the solvent, will, in…' which makes for very slow and fragmented reading, distracting the reader from the content. The best, and highly amusing, discussion of punctuation is in Lynne Truss's *Eats, Shoots & Leaves: Why, Commas Really Do Make a Difference!* William Strunk's classic *The Elements of Style* is also a rather good guide. There are now even illustrated editions of both I see.

Then there's the 'Oxford comma', or 'serial comma', which seems to cause endless debate in the US, but few care about it in its homeland, other than its originators, OUP. For a definition, examples and amusing debate on it, see The Great Oxford Comma Debate.[21] The Associated Press's editor concludes excellently, with the last word on the issue. Well worth a read.

---

[21] https://muckrack.com/blog/2022/05/04/oxford-comma

Capitals all over! As an editor, one sometimes wonders if authors have some kind of obsession with 'capitalism' or 'capitals of the world'. Or perhaps have been very influenced by German, which capitalises all nouns. Some authors do seem to think that everything in their field deserves a capital because of its perceived importance. In particular, subject areas like 'history' are never capitalised, the only exceptions being languages, 'Setswana' for example. Reading also becomes discontinuous, for an English reader at least. Capitals, like punctuation, are visual 'flags' to the reader. The case here is definitely for the minimalist approach: all capitalization needs a good reason for its use: proper nouns, names, and languages, yes, but little else. A publisher will, however, have 'house style' rules for capitalization of headings and publication titles (see below for house style).

Dictionaries and correct spelling must, one need hardly say, be in the armoury of every author. Almost all academic authors use a word processor[22] which has a spell checker, but technical, specialist and non-English words will not be included. A trap that I have found too many authors falling into is the language of the spelling and grammar checker. (See more in the section below, under 'Technical aspects'....) When it comes to *specialist vocabulary*, it is very much the author's responsibility to ensure correct spelling. It is, after all, the author, and not the editor, who is more specialised in the subject area. Lack of consistency will be a red flag to an editor though.

A manuscript that has not even been spell-checked with a word processor's tool, will leave a very poor impression of the author, and probably lead to rejection, immediately. Also, see the above in the main text section on gender bias, racism, neglect of minority interests, prejudged attitudes, and unsubstantiated allegations

---

[22] Some authors may use LaTeX, and this is beyond my scope or knowledge, but some publishers do accept LaTeX manuscripts. I do love their statement, "...in most typesetting or word-processing systems, the author would have to decide what layout to use, so would select (say) 18pt Times Roman for the title, 12pt Times Italic for the name, and so on. This has two results: authors wasting their time with designs; and a lot of badly designed documents!" From 'An introduction to LaTeX' at https://www.latex-project.org/about/. That writer, however, doesn't seem to know about paragraph styles.

House style

House style: *-zations and –sations:* what is correct English? Your spell checker may not help here.

Because of the vagaries of English grammar and spelling, publishers usually have their own sets of rules to clarify ambiguities, their 'house style'. Individual publishers will have their individual in-house style guides, but many follow that of others. The commonest in the US are the

AN EXAMPLE OF PART OF A PUBLISHER'S HOUSE STYLE

paragraph look right or author uses consistently; never ten%. (Percent is American.)

10. Measures/Units
2.3 cm, (i.e., space between the number and the unit).
6487 ms^{-1} for academic and higher school levels, but if author uses m/s style retain this.
For lower school (up to Form 3) use m/s.
Km^2 not sq.km.
thirty-three square kilometres: no other alternatives.

11. Dates and Time
3 July 1951
Sunday 3rd July 1951 (i.e., if day is in)
Never July 3, 1951 or 3rd July 1951
3/7/51, i.e., date, month year
In the 1920s not 1920's., unless poseessive as in "a 1920's tune"
1945–46 (not 1945-1946 or 1945 - 6) but if you use 'to' instead of the en dash then you must include the whole number, e.g., 'From 1986 to 1991, he taught at the university.' (See 14 below.)
AD 1500 or 900 BC. Use small caps for AD and BC (same for CE and BCE), and space between.
15.00hrs, 3 o'clock, 6 p.m. (include stops)

12. Page numbers
126–7 (not 126-27), or 126–7 (not 126-137). (See 14 below.)

13. Money
P15.30, £2.50, i.e., no spaces. Pula, Rand, Pound (caps)

14. em – and en — rules (British style)
en dash with no space if meaning "to", e.g., "2018–19" (if it looks better put "to" in its place).
en dash with spaces where subclause are being defined: "…in fact – if this is true – all are lies and deceit"
em dash only used for special cases.
(*Do not use* the Economist's use of Americn styles for em usage: "…in fact—if this is true—all are lies and deceit".)

15. Lists
Numbering:
1. (Full stops after Arabic numbers: preferably, all Roman to align right)
  (a)
  (b)
  (c)
    (i)
    (ii)
    (iii)

"… as follows" is always followed by a colon and thereafter semi-colons till at

Chicago Manual of Style, the MLA Handbook, the generic APA, the Elements of Style, and, mostly for journalists, AP Styles. These are available in MS Word. In the UK, the New Oxford Style Manual is popular, An individual publisher's house style will determine the degree to which British and American (or other) English are used. This is particularly relevant for transatlantic publishers.

A publisher's house style will also cover every aspect of text formatting. These will include fonts, leading, indentation, headings and so on. (See facing page for a good example.)

The author would usefully be familiar with at least one of these, but need not be overly concerned at manuscript stage, especially if the author is still looking for a publisher. Consistency is your best guide.

Technical aspects: computer hazards: well, just a few of them

(a) The first is the *spell checker*. These are very useful for a general scan, and for terrible 'typists' like me, an absolute godsend. The entire document needs to be selected and then the language chosen. It's really important to select the correct version of English for your whole manuscript. Otherwise your checker will not work in the right way. Some copied and pasted text may have used a different language dictionary (usually this is with US and UK versions). Secondly, beware of the *custom dictionary*. One can easily add incorrect words to this, and thereafter the incorrectly spelt word will always appear as correct. So it's worth knowing how to check the contents of the custom dictionary. Thirdly, the dictionary will not usually contain specialist vocabulary, and consistency in this area needs careful proof-checking. Word hyphenation is a particular case in point.

When I was running a workshop for writers in Ethiopia, I asked whether they use British or American English, I was told that they don't mind either. I didn't pursue the matter further but have always wondered what an English exam paper might look like! On looking further now, I found that "Ethiopian English is neither codified nor seems to follow a particular variety".[23] So Ethiopian English definitely doesn't have a spell-checker.

(b) Grammar checkers have been coming into their own in recent years, with Grammarly and ProWritingAid leading the pack. They can be of limited use to the academic, specialist writer, but can make useful suggestions and pick up some more obvious serious errors. Whereas they can provide a very useful first-run edit, I still have to go through every manuscript again after experimentally using them, so often think it was a waste of my time. A professional human editor sees very much more than even the best of these tools. Some editors may use the professional software PerfectIt for consistency and style checks. So what about AI, we all ask. Well, to date the very best seem very far off the mark. Finally, do leave any spell or grammar checkers off during writing – they can distract from your creative flow.

(c) Rearranging of text is one of the most powerful word-processing tools. With a simple *cut and paste,* material is moved from one section to another. There are two dangers here, both of which I see repeatedly occurring in manuscripts. Firstly, the material has been copied instead of cut, thus leaving the original in place, and so duplicating the material in another place. One version then gets changed whilst the other does not, leaving a non-exact duplicate. The perhaps more serious error is that the flow of the material is disrupted. For example, if the piece cut is pasted earlier, it may involve terms, ideas or concepts that have not yet been covered. Sorting this out is an editorial nightmare and will lead to frustration all round later. And then there's the content that's been copied from another source, but has a bad error in it. I recently saw a paragraph stating something about the 'prime minister' in a country that has a president instead – clearly pasted from elsewhere. The pasted copy can also read differently in writing style, making the manuscript uneven.

(d) Another wonderfully powerful tool is the *search and replace* facility. But if the logic is not carefully followed, then all forms of disaster can take place. For example, changing 'air' to 'atmosphere' and clicking

---

[23] English in Ethiopia: https://eric.ed.gov/?id=EJ1146434

'change all' will lead to marvellous new words like 'fatmosphere' for 'fair'.[24] So diligent use of 'whole word only' and 'match case' is crucial.

(e) The next myth, a real trap, is that *the author can design the type and the pages*. Typical is the academic who comes to his or her friend, the publisher, editor or typesetter and says, "But I have all the same software as you, even newer versions. Why can't I make my pages look as good as you do? Can't you give me a few lessons?". To which the response will probably be, "Well, maybe next week" – for the next five years. A great many academics spend (or waste!) vast amounts of their time trying to hand over to publishers what they think is printable, and just needs 'a little bit' of editing, 'tidying up' ('…five of my colleagues have been through it'). And the first thing the publisher will do is rip out all those weeks or months of formatting because the author's version is full of so many conflicting or unusable paragraph styles. See however, 'Text and formatting: paragraph styles' in the next chapter. The only real case for an author spending such time on formatting is with in-house-produced journals *that have a style guide*. And it is invariably a thankless job – the academic isn't paid for it, and the *real cost in time spent*, in terms of what an academic is paid (in relative terms), is very high.

(f) Then there's *the multiple version problem*, although I've seen less of this in recent years with academics. This can happen when multiple devices are used and not properly synchronised. Moving from office desktop to home laptop and cafe iPad is where this happens. A common one is with Dropbox, which shows an alternate version where the same document has been worked on using different machines. MS Word produces a 'recovered' file after a crash, and there is ambiguity about which version to use.

> **Tip::** So check the 'date last modified' of the file if you want to be sure of the right one.

(g) The last word in computer hazards is *lost data*. There have been endless appalling cases where months and years of work have been lost due to lack of electronic backup. Perhaps the saddest is that of the university's IT department expert who came into an author's office, and the author then related: "I said I had a real problem, so they reformatted

---

[24] My spell checker originally wanted to change 'fatmosphere' back to 'atmosphere'.

my drive and reinstalled the system. The computer now works fine". The rest was lost in a bucketful of tears…. Backing up, remotely, online, as well as to an external drive, need to be part of any writer's daily toolkit. Failing to back up will never receive anyone's sympathy. Then there's the horror of your laptop being stolen….

Textbooks

Consideration needs to be given to a special case of academic writing, *the textbook* or *course book*. Many authors have found a specific demand and gap in the market for a single volume that covers course content, either at tertiary or lower levels. In large market areas, schools particularly, publishers will normally commission writers after seeing a large (but very competitive) market potential. But with tertiary institutions, there is often a real and valid need to have a single course book, rather than expecting students to purchase several books, possibly imported or very expensive, or both. Rarely will original research will be required for textbooks, but a great deal of time and thought must go into presentation and methodology. Originality is still a very strong requirement.

For the academic, textbook writing is a specialised mode of writing. In a good many ways it is quite different. This is especially true of school textbooks where knowledge, interpretation, application and use of language and conceptual levels are critical.

For both school and tertiary level books, there are some key differences to bear in mind when being approached by a publisher, or submitting a proposal. The arrangement of the content will have to interpret and follow a syllabus to start with. The content will also have to be split into manageable sections. Illustrations are essential and heavily used in most cases. You need to either provide or write design or artist briefs for them.

This topic is really beyond the scope of this monograph, but from my years of textbook publishing, and if you would like to pursue this route, do get in touch. There's a useful article for academics here: Why it is so hard for academics to write textbooks.[25] Nonetheless, some fine academics make the switch quite easily, and even write fiction.

---

[25] https://www.researchgate.net/publication/367084115_Why_it_is_so_hard_for_academics_to_write_textbooks

HEALTHY LIVING

UNIT 7.1
PERSONAL HYGIENE: LOOKING AFTER YOUR BODY

Ideas and Concepts for the Student
- Personal hygiene is essential if the body is to be maintained in good health.
- Different parts of the body naturally carry a number of different types of microbes. Personal hygiene involves keeping the skin, exposed organs and clothes clean to ensure that the numbers of microbes is kept to a minimum.
- Certain parts of the body such as around the reproductive organs need special attention because they provide microbes with an excellent environment in which to live and reproduce.

Core Background for the Teacher
The outer surface of the body is broken by a number of openings into the inner body and it also holds some delicate and very important organs, all of which have to be looked after carefully to prevent infection and disease.

Skin
The skin forms the first defence barrier against infection and also serves the function of retaining water inside the tissues of the body. The skin is made up of two layers: an outer epidermis and an inner layer called the dermis. The epidermis is composed of three layers of cells. The outer protective layer of the epidermis is formed by flat overlapping dead cells which are constantly being shed and replaced. These cells are covered with a fatty film which provides the skin with a waterproof covering. The next layer called the granular layer is made up of a mixture of living and dead cells and it covers the innermost layer of the epidermis called the Malphighian layer.

FIG 7.1: CROSS SECTION OF THE SKIN

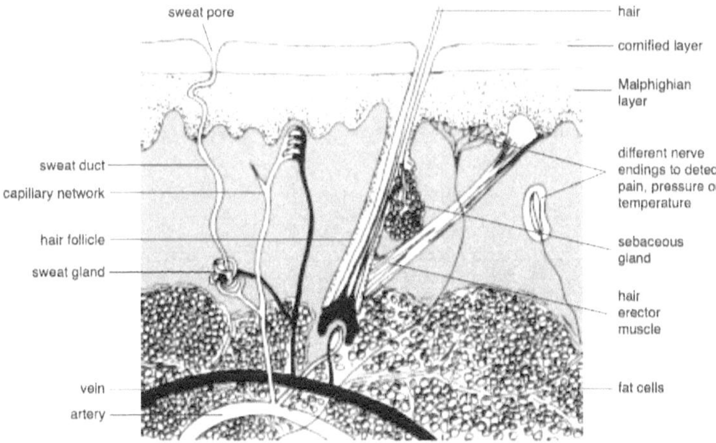

Chapter 6.
PREPARING YOUR MANUSCRIPT FOR SUBMISSION FOR PUBLICATION

With submissions. publishers vary in the way they want manuscripts presented, [26] but there are some very good ground rules that almost every publisher will follow.

General points

Few, if any, publishers are now prepared to accept any manuscript that is not already digital. Use headers and footers effectively in your manuscript. Make sure they contain your name, contact details, manuscript title, date and page numbers.

Text and formatting: paragraph styles

Authors need not be overmuch concerned with formatting their manuscripts, as this will be almost certainly changed by the publisher. What the publisher wants is clarity of instruction.

But, the best formatting information by far that you can give the publisher is by consistently using paragraph styles. These are built into MS Word and almost every other word processor. Every non-fiction writer of any kind needs these skills. Your publisher is on your side straight away, at least seeing them well used. Badly used, they are a disaster. Learn how to use them. Consistently. At the minimum, learn to use styles for text, headings, and quotations.

> **Tip::** make sure that the first paragraph under a heading is not indented, as in this book. Why? Otherwise it looks terrible. Make a paragraph style to speed things up.

If you really don't want to learn or use styles, just double-space everything, and make *very* sure your headings are properly clear, unambiguous and hierarchical. It is generally best to aim for a maximum of three levels below the chapter heading, leaving a fourth one for exceptional cases. More than three levels of heading below the chapter

---

[26] See Chapter 8 for individual publishers' submission guidelines.

heading *may* indicate a poorly structured manuscript. Ebooks often allow fewer. Each heading level has its own style.

The font and type size that the author (or Word!) uses will probably bear little resemblance to that of the final book. If the author has properly used paragraph styles, the publisher's typesetter or designer will modify the styles according to the book's specifications. If the author does not use styles, the typesetter, on instructions from the publisher or editor, will specify them for text, headings, quotations and references, as well as for all table and graph titles, and more. The author also needs to give a clear indication of italics and bold words or phrases.

Tables

Very large tables – with very many columns or rows – may be difficult to fit on a page or pair of facing pages. There are always ways around this, and don't let the publisher, editor or page designer bully you into having to delete your data. But, having said that, you will need to be accommodating as to how the table fits. A good relationship with your editor will be useful

Charts and graphs

You need to have generated these from a spreadsheet. The publisher will standardise the look and feel of these, so the author will *have to* provide the original data, in tables, for all charts or graphs. Unless your book will be produced in colour (expensive printing), ensure that each line/bar or other representation is clearly distinguishable using black, greys and dotted or dashed lines. See overleaf for good black and grey usage.

Photos and drawings

Photos need to be eventually presented to the publisher in their originals. One of the commonest errors that authors make is putting their scanned images into a word processing application and thinking that is it, without keeping the originals. Print resolution, however, needs to be high, and the scan needs to be separately provided. Initially, on manuscript submission, low-resolution scans or photocopies will suffice, however.

> **Tip::** You may be able to export your drawing or photo as an html web page. You can then see your illustrations in their full format, as imported, before Word compresses them. Different versions of Word vary as to how you do this. It is far easier if you keep the originals however.

An example page with tables and charts.

COORDINATION OF MACROECONOMIC POLICIES IN THE SOUTHERN AFRICAN DEVELOPMENT COMMUNITY REGION

TABLE 4: DESCRIPTIVE STATISTICS MEASURING THE DEGREE OF ECONOMIC CONVERGENCE IN SADC - AVERAGE ANNUAL INFLATION

Period	Mean	Std. Dev.
1992 - 1996[1]	24.17	7.55
1997 - 2002[2]	14.70	3.57
2002 - 2006[3]	10.69	6.25
2007 - 2011[3]	9.96	3.19

Notes:

1. Excluding Angola, DRC, Lesotho, Mozambique and Tanzania

2. Excluding Angola, DRC, Lesotho and Tanzania

3. Excluding Angola and Zimbabwe

indicates a decreasing variation of inflation among the SADC countries; Chart 1 (a). Thus, data suggests that SADC countries are not only converging but converging towards the set targets.

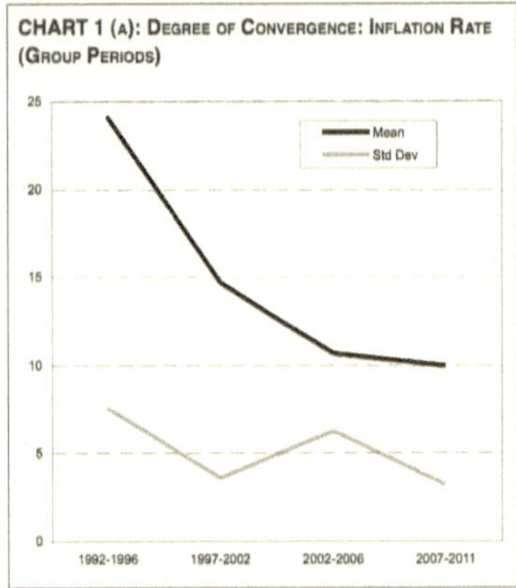

CHART 1 (A): DEGREE OF CONVERGENCE: INFLATION RATE (GROUP PERIODS)

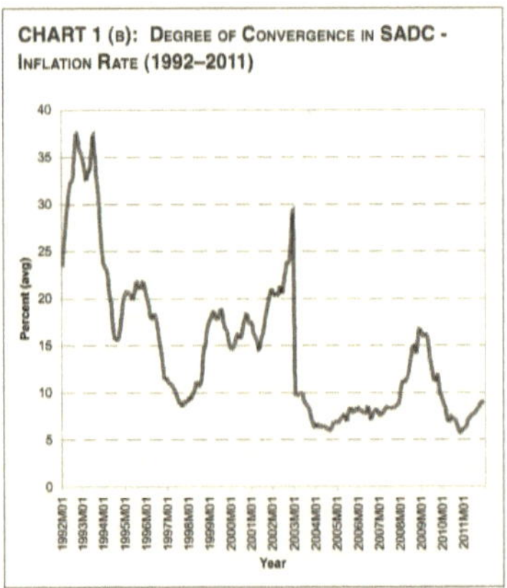

CHART 1 (B): DEGREE OF CONVERGENCE IN SADC - INFLATION RATE (1992–2011)

B. Fiscal Policy

5.1.2 Budget Balance/GDP

The study uses the cash surplus/deficit as a ratio of GDP measure fiscal policy coordination and convergence in SADC. Fiscal data are similarly grouped into four 5-year periods (owing to the unavailability of more recent data, which end before 2009 for most countries, data for two years prior to the formation of SADC are added; therefore the data set starts from 1990 to 2009). Unlike the inflation data series, which were easily available, obtaining the budget (surplus/deficit)/GDP data was a challenge for most countries. Data were not available for Angola, Malawi, Mozambique, Swaziland and Zimbabwe. Of the remaining nine countries where data were obtained, the data series for DRC was rejected by the analysis as containing fatal errors, while that of Namibia was found to be integrated of order I (1). The data series for Zambia was only available up to 1999 and, hence, Zambia was left out of the analysis. Therefore, data for only six countries was used for analysis during the first three 5-year periods, being Botswana, Lesotho, Mauritius, Seychelles, RSA and Tanzania. Moreover, the tail end of the last group (2004 – 2009) comprised only four countries, as the data series for both Tanzania and Seychelles ended in 2005. The results are shown in Table 5 and Charts 2(a) and 2(b).

The mean of the budget balance/GDP ratio rises from -1.18 for the period 1990 – 1994 to 1.68 during 1995 to 1999 and subsequently declines. The standard deviation indicates a reduction in variation of budget performance, therefore progress towards convergence. Overall, there has been transition from budget deficit to surplus position for the countries included in the analysis. The deterioration in the latter period and increased variation could be attributed to the impact of the 2002 – 2008 economic crisis.

TABLE 5: DESCRIPTIVE STATISTICS MEASURING THE DEGREE OF ECONOMIC CONVERGENCE IN SADC – PUBLIC SURPLUS/ DEFICIT AS A PERCENTAGE OF GDP

Period	Mean	Std. Dev.
1990 - 1994	-1.18	1.74
1995 - 1999	1.68	1.76
2000 - 2004	1.01	1.38
2005 - 2009[1]	1.08	4.40

Note:1. The last 5-year period group comprises only 4 countries due to lack of data.

5.1.3 Public Debt/GDP

Analysis of public debt/GDP ratio uses annual data from 1992 to 2011 and includes eight countries for which data were available, namely: Botswana, Lesotho, Malawi, Namibia, RSA, Tanzania, Zambia and Zimbabwe. As indicated in Charts 3(a), 3(b) and Table 6, the debt ratio was highest in the mid-1990s but fell sharply thereafter, before declining towards the set criteria. Thus, countries have been taking measures to reduce debt, including through support by development partners and multilateral agencies. However, variability of debt/GDP data is substantial (low degree of convergence) as shown by large standard deviation.

Line drawings may be provided by the author. The same applies as for photos to any original work presented.

The publisher will have a contractual clause stating lack of liability for any loss of your material – by whatever cause. You must keep a backup, both on a local drive and remotely. In the case of printed materials, I recommend at least a photocopy, or preferably a good high resolution scan.

Maps

New maps are often generated by specialist mapping software. The author will need to ensure that these are saved in high-resolution PNG, JPG or EPS format. A copy of the original mapping software file needs to be backed up carefully. The author needs to be aware that any size reduction due to the book format will also reduce the lettering size, so this should be carefully watched out for. One cannot simply expect a glorious full-colour A2 map to be reduced to A5 (one-eighth of the size) and expect to be able to read the place names. The sizes of the maps will need to be agreed with the publisher at a later stage and probably redrawn to match the specification. Hence the importance of keeping the data files.

Permissions and copyright

An author's publishing contract will always contain a clause absolving the publisher from all liability for copyright infringement, libel and slander. These are fairly standard. What the author must ensure is that permission has been obtained for any copyright material used in the manuscript. As noted above, plagiarism can become an issue. Short quotes for argument or critique, with 'fair usage' do not require permission, although there is always a debate on the meaning of 'short': consult your editor. In essence, your quotes need to support your thesis, not using them as your own work. It is essential that such material is always in quotation marks or indented, and sources are *fully* stated. This may also apply to tables of data.

With artwork of any kind from another source, the copyright owner will fight shy of giving permission to use in any book that is non-print, digital in any form. It's just too easy to steal digital work. So you may have to drop such artwork from your digital edition.

Bigger publishers may well have 'permissions' departments, but many will respond that you either have to pay for the permissions service, or provide you with a standard permissions request form for you to use. In either case, you will have to track down the copyright owner. When writing it is crucial, therefore, that you keep a note of, and acknowledge your sources of copyright material – anything that you have not produced. This includes material that may be owned by the successors of the original writer or artist. Occasionally, where I have been unable to track down a copyright owner, often of rare, obscure or ancient illustrations, I have put in a sentence on the copyright page saying that every effort has been made to contact the copyright owner, and that if we are contacted by such, we would be happy to pay the permission fee. It hardly needs saying, but you need to be on very solid ground with a statement like that: you could get badly burnt, or be prepared to go to court. It will be the author's liability, naturally, as the illustration is in the author's work.

AI introduces new difficulties for writers. Determining whether a particular source has involved AI in its creation can be quite challenging. It becomes crucial to exercise additional diligence when citing sources under fair usage conditions. This ensures that any potential legal claims of plagiarism or copyright infringement can be effectively addressed and resolved.[27]

> Of course, illegal copying has always been around, long before the digital age. I once encountered a situation in a photocopying shop and found a teacher copying pages from a mathematics series I had published. I felt I had better say something, so I walked over to her, said I was the publisher, and that what she was doing was not right. The young woman was embarrassed and left hastily. I never followed that up in any way. No doubt she was a volunteer at a very poor school, so what the hell! She had nothing to gain from this personally. By comparison, an author friend of mine had his maths textbooks copied on a huge scale and sold in Nigeria. These are the big fish of copyright infringement who need pursuing. Writers do suffer badly from copyright infringement, as do musicians and fine artists.

The index, first stage

It is best to give some thought to an index at an early stage in your writing. It will add value, and may be essential for an academic work. Some academic books may not *require* indexing: conference proceedings

---

[27] This paragraph and the next include suggestions from ChatGPT.

A WELL-FORMED INDEX FROM A PROFESSIONAL

130   **P**atrick   van   **r**ensburg: *AnnotatedBibliography*

and multi-author works, for example, are sometimes not indexed (despite being invaluable to a reader, and adding value to the work).

By the time you have finalised your manuscript, you should also be prepared to, soon after, produce a list of the words and phrases you want indexed. Proper names are the simplest words to index, including people and places, company names, chemical elements, names of vessels, Latin names for living things, stars and planets. Only you (or a very committed editor) can specify the words you want in the index, however.

> **How to tip:** In your word processor, you may like to mark each index entry to produce your list. For example, use underlining or colouring, or using any format that your manuscript does not otherwise use. If, say, you have coloured all index words or phrases red, then you can search for all black words and replace them with a space (or a special character like ^ or ±). After that, all that will remain will be your indexed entries which you can sort alphabetically. You can also use Character Styles in Word to speed up the process.

> **Another tip:** Well, get rid of all those extra spaces (or a special characters) first of course – a judicious search and replace will manage that in a minute or two. Just don't delete the lot. You can eventually replace the spaces with hard paragraph returns for a good and sortable list.

It is not necessary to produce your list of indexable words or phrases with the manuscript, and it will be worth getting further guidance from your publisher once the manuscript is under consideration. But, sooner or later, you will need to do it. It is essential that your index word list exists, at the very latest, by the time page proofs are on their way. Otherwise you may not have time and hold up publication. So, do not leave this until the last minute.

MS Word, and other software, can produce an index for your manuscript. They can be tricky to use, though. Professional indexing can be rather expensive for most academic authors, and it is very unlikely that the publisher will produce, or pay for, the index. But, as with professional editing, an indexer will produce a much better index. Indexers are highly skilled and will handle cross-referencing and sublevels of an index in hierarchical form, for example.

Author information

The *editorial information form* is a most useful publisher's tool. It may be given to an author before the manuscript is completed, in response to a proposal, on handover of the manuscript, or even during the review process. Key questions will be asked of the author relating to all aspects of the manuscript. These can include author details, cover ideas and blurb, progress and timelines for the main text, illustrations, tables and the in-

AN EXAMPLE OF PART OF AN AUTHOR'S EDITORIAL INFORMATION FORM

For the below please indicate what you are providing.

(f)	Dedication	YES/NO or N/A	(l)	List of Maps	YES/NO or N/A
(g)	Contents List	YES/NO	(m)	List of Tables	YES/NO or N/A
(h)	Foreword	YES/NO or N/A	(n)	List of Abbreviations	YES/NO or N/A
(i)	Preface	YES/NO	(o)	Notes on the Contributors	YES/NO or N/A
(j)	Acknowledgements	YES/NO or N/A	(p)	Introduction	YES/NO or N/A
(k)	List of Illustrations	YES/NO or N/A	(q)	Any other preliminary matter	YES/NO (If YES, please specify what below.)

3. ENDMATTER

For the below please indicate what you are providing.

(a)	Appendixes	YES/NO or N/A	(c)	References	YES/NO or N/A
(b)	Endnotes	YES/NO or N/A	(d)	Bibliography	YES/NO

(e) Any other endmatter YES/NO (Please specify what, if YES.)

(f) Chapter headings may appear at the top of the page as running headlines. If chapter titles are more than 50 characters in length they will require abbreviation. Please supply the preferred shortened forms of chapter headings over 50 characters.

4. THE MAIN TEXT

Please confirm that the manuscript is **complete**. YES/NO

If it is not, please list any items which are to follow, and indicate their approximate length and word count, and when they will reach us.

Item   Length (Pages)   Word count   Likely Delivery Date

Please confirm that the manuscript is identical on disc and the printout (if provided). YES/NO N/A

Does the manuscript include **tables**? YES/NO If so, how many?

Are any tables likely to cause special difficulty (e.g., particularly large, more than half a page)? YES/NO On which pages do they occur/what are their numbers?

Does the manuscript include **charts**? YES/NO If so, how many?

All chart data will be required in MS Excel. Is the chart data available? YES/NO

Are any charts likely to cause special difficulty (e.g., more than four categories)? YES/NO On which pages do they occur/what are their numbers?

dex. Copyright and libel issues may also be addressed. Careful and full responses are expected of the author. Incomplete answers may cause breaks in schedules later, cause delays in publication, or rejection.

The effects of production processes and technology on manuscript preparation

The medium for almost all manuscripts is digital. From the software point of view, the *de facto* standard for text has become Microsoft Word, but any text software that can produce RTF files is fine. Most graphs or charts, and many tables, are often produced in Microsoft Excel, and all publishers will be able to read these either is .xls or .csv formats. Also see the footnote 22 on LaTeX, on page 15.

Two problem areas of graphics are frequently encountered by publishers. The first relates to graphs or other data embedded in a word-processing document. It is critical that the original data or drawing files are included. Graphs often need redrawing to size and style, whilst photos and drawings need resizing at print-quality resolutions.[28] for print. If unsure, go higher, and consult your publisher, or potential publisher, of course. Also see the section in Chapter 6, page 23.

Not so long ago 'digital' used to refer to five-and-a-quarter-inch floppy discs, three-and-a-half inch ones, CD-R, CD-RW and flash drives with USB interfaces. I have a mini-museum for most of those. Going even further back I have had handwritten manuscripts typed onto a floppy disc. Compare that to now, when it is normal practice to submit via a cloud upload, or by email. It looks as if the former will remain the submission method of choice for a good while, yet.

---

[28] Far too many authors expect that they can get printouts from what they see on screen. A minimum resolution of 150 dpi for photos and 300 dpi for line artwork are essential. A starter test is to print out on a home printer or blow up the picture on screen.

Chapter 7.
FINDING A PUBLISHER

Looking in bookshops and libraries for books that are similar to yours (and hopefully not the same) can be a very useful exercise. A good bookshop or library, on the street or online, can be easier to browse than flogging through endless websites. After that, you can look for the publishers' sites. The *Writers and Artists Yearbook* may also help in your selection.[29]

You will want to find a publisher who will enhance your academic career, whether it be in terms of promotion, peer reputation or finding a new post. Also, look for evidence that a publisher can promote your book well.

✓ An excellent source of over 500 global academic publishers is at the Academic Publishers' Directory.[30]

✓ Covering mostly UK and US publishers, this list of 'top 36' also includes some from India, Canada and Australia: Reedsy top 36.[31] Of these 23 also publish ebooks. Most of the publishers listed accept submissions of unsolicited manuscripts.

✓ In the US, 115 academic publishers are at Academic Publishers' Directory of United States.[32]

✓ Also in the US, the Association of University Presses Directory[33] provides all US academic publishers, by subscription, but they have a free download of publishers by subject area at their Press Subject Area Grid.[34]

✓ In the UK, the biggest source of 78 academic publishers is at Academic Publishers' Directory of the United Kingdom.[35]

---

[29] Also see Luey (2009) for more on this.

[30] https://www.publishersglobal.com/directory/subject/academic-publishers

[31] https://blog.reedsy.com/publishers/academic/

[32] https://blog.reedsy.com/publishers/academic/

[33] https://aupresses.org/membership/annual-directory/

[34] https://aupresses.org/resources/aupresses-subject-area-grid/

[35] https://www.publishersglobal.com/directory/united-kingdom/subject/academic-publishers

The only problem with some of these lists is the non-inclusion of some of the major non-university presses such as Palgrave, Pearson, W.W. Norton, and the Big Five – Macmillan, Hachette, Penguin Random House, HarperCollins and Simon & Schuster. All have academic arms. They are mostly multinational with all the market advantages that these have for authors.

It is also worth checking the publishers in the reviews sections of journals in your field. These can give you leads as to which publishers may be interested in your manuscript.

Finally, do ask your colleagues and friends too. Have any been published recently? What were their experiences? Do they have good contact with an acquisitions editor or publisher? Word of mouth can be very useful, even in the digital age.

Chapter 8.
INDIVIDUAL PUBLISHERS' SUBMISSION GUIDELINES

Publishers' submission guidelines vary considerably, so it is essential to read them before submitting your proposal or manuscript. Some will refer you to a specific acquisitions editor. None of the below examples says that they do not accept unsolicited proposals or manuscripts.

✓ Bloomsbury: 'Submitting a Book Proposal' https://www.bloomsbury.com/uk/discover/bloomsbury-academic/authors/submitting-a-book-proposal/

✓ Routledge: 'Submit your book proposal' https://www.routledge.com/our-customers/authors/submit-your-book-proposal

✓ OUP Academic: 'Submitting a proposal' https://academic.oup.com/pages/authoring/books/submitting-a-proposal

✓ OUP also has the 64-page 'A Handbook for Authors: Preparing Your Manuscript for Oxford University Press'.

✓ Palgrave Macmillan: 'Submit a Proposal' https://www.palgrave.com/gp/book-authors/publishing-guidelines/submit-a-proposal

✓ MIT Press: 'Submitting a Book Proposal' https://mitpress.mit.edu/submitting-book-proposal/

✓ UC Press: 'Book Proposal Guidelines' https://www.ucpress.edu/resources/book-proposal-guidelines

✓ MSU Press: 'Submission Guidelines' https://msupress.org/author-information/current-authors/submission-guidelines/

✓ One World Publications: 'Book Proposals' https://oneworld-publications.com/about/book-proposals/?wpv-child-of=33

Chapter 9.
Manuscript accepted!

At last your manuscript has been accepted by a publisher. Now begins another journey.

...or provisionally, or 'salvageable'

A publisher, possibly through their acquisitions editor, may make a provisional offer to publish, in a 'letter of intent', but with conditions attached. The in-house term is 'salvageable', meaning publishable if the author can rework parts of the manuscript, and be offered the option of 'developmental editing'. This would involve working with a development editor to get the manuscript in shape, before any other kind of editing takes place. This can take time. I have worked with authors whose manuscripts were full of promise: some took over six months and another two years to get into shape.

Getting your contract

Once you have an initial agreement with a publisher, you should receive the letter of intent indicating willingness to publish. This will have basic conditions in it, in particular royalties, and manuscript final delivery. It may take a while to draw up the contract, possibly following discussion of details with you, so this initial letter is a holding commitment. The contract will then usually be offered in a few weeks and should reflect the discussions you have had with the acquisitions editor or publisher. Read it through carefully, and you may wish to consult with other authors, a lawyer, colleagues or friends. You will be expected to have read and understood the contract before you sign it. If you have any difficulties, spell them out to the publisher clearly. There are legally binding obligations on both parties. One of them is that the copyright, for the duration of the contract, is assigned to the publisher. This avoids a situation of an author publishing with more than one publisher simultaneously.

On royalties

Although it was beyond the original scope of this monograph, I shall include this fairly complex area since it is often asked about by authors. So, it is worth mentioning a few points, even at the risk of being somewhat simplistic. There are usually two types of royalty payment: 'on receipts' and 'on published price'.

Publishers may well prefer 'on receipts' as it is much easier to monitor from an accounting point of view, and covers special deals, discounts and exports cleanly. What it means is that whatever the publisher sells a copy of a book for, the author gets a specific percentage of that amount. Royalties on 'published price' (the bookshop retail price) can be tricky to determine as booksellers or distributors may well not stick to what the publisher has recommended, and on export sales this is impossible to monitor.

Authors may also be offered 'scaled' royalties, whereby royalties will be low on the first sales and thereafter increase to a higher level. Authors of academic books with small print runs will find that royalties are very low, or zero in the case of OA. The plain fact is that academic authors should not generally expect to rely on publishing royalties as a source of income.

The exceptions are not academic books, per se, but popularised books by academics, often in the sciences, such as Carl Sagan's *Cosmos*. One should definitely not think that Stephen Hawking's bestseller *A Brief History of Time* is replicable. In the humanities and social sciences Yuval Noah Harari's *Sapiens: A Brief History of Humankind*, and Stephen J. Levitt et *al.*'s *Freakonomics: A Rogue Economist Explores the Hidden Side of Everything* are good examples. Another academic-based series, covering many fields is *Introducing Graphic Guides*.[36] This sort of publication is beyond the scope of this work, however.

The exponential effect of royalty increases on price: adding another 5% to the royalty will increase the price by very much more than this and might well put the book out of the market in terms of price. If arguing royalties, authors should be aware that the standard figure of 10% (maybe 15% on receipts) exists for sound historical business reasons and not as a conspiracy among publishers for ripping off authors. It is, for example, much better to sell 2000 copies (with a 5% royalty) at a price of £10 (£1000) than 10% of 500 copies at £13 (£650) where the £10 price has been determined as all the 'market will bear'. But that is another essay or monograph in itself.

It is worth noting that booksellers, through their distributors, take between 30% and 60% of the retail price. Then there are all the design, layout and editing costs. Printing is a large factor also, and is variable,

---

[36] https://www.introducingbooks.com/

depending on print run, with very large economies of scale. Low print runs lead to high prices, and this is especially relevant to academic books where a 5% royalty is common. The publisher's share may be as little as 10%, or even a loss, if the printed book does not sell and just takes up warehouse space. Print on demand, where books are printed to order often as single copies, costs are also high.

A note on ebook royalties, especially for the self-published author. Amazon's highest royalty is 70%. But that is only for a very limited book price range, $3 to $5 as I write, and not for all countries. It drops to 35% for many countries, and outside that price range. There is also a 'minimum price' factor which reduces this dramatically for lower-priced books. Apple pays 70% on everything, Added to that is the US 30% tax that Amazon says it is obliged to withhold from non-US residents, which takes 70% down to 49%, 35% to 24.5%, unless the country (including the UK) has a bilateral tax agreement with the US. For US resident taxpayers, as well as those wishing to reclaim their 30% against expenses, there will be tax forms to complete. The withholding tax *may* apply with any American company that you use.

Distributors will take their 10% or so. Lulu, in its global mode, shows in detail the royalties accrued for each of its distributors in impressive detail.

Open Access

Open access (OA) started in the early 2000s, with journals. It spread rapidly, notably in Latin America. The concept involves making current and past research widely available under Creative Commons (CC) licenses. The debate has been ongoing, and has even been described as the wild west of academic publishing, although the matter appears to be resolving itself to some degree as more publishers sign up to the OA model. A three-year investigative programme in the UK, reported on OA in great detail at The Academic Book of the Future,[37] which has an accompanying book. Wikipedia's OA article shows over 280 citation footnotes, making up over half of the 47 pages of the article. The debate has had two fairly polarised sides. One of the main issues is that authors do not receive royalties, but conversely their exposure and potential for citation is far greater than with the traditional publishing model.

---

[37] https://academicbookfuture.org/

So, what exactly is OA, and what are the implications for the academic author of books and monographs?

Springer Nature defines it thus: "Open access (OA) refers to the free, immediate, online availability of research outputs such as journal articles or books, combined with the rights to use these outputs fully in the digital environment. OA content is open to all, with no access fees". This comes along with CC licensing of six types for books. These vary as to whether credit must be given to the author, copyright retained, commercial use permitted, adaptation and any usage permitted. They have a symbol such as, this commonly used one indicating author attribution, non-commercial usage, and no derivatives or adaptations. The full list is at About CC Licenses.[38] All OA books need to have one of these six.

Government research funders in numerous countries (including all of the EU) stipulate that the research they fund be published via OA. The very up-to-date Open Access Policy of the UK Research and Innovation site[39] spells out conditions and advice in great detail. The Directory of Open Access Books[40] lists peer-reviewed academic books published in various Open Access formats. This is searchable by publisher and subject, so can be used to find suitable publishers for submission of proposals. The site also has many other OA resources. The Internet Archive[41] also has a massive collection of digital books, and much more.

So how does this work in practice? Well, there are 18 listed business models,[42] including crowdfunding and volunteer effort. But a realistic, long-term viable solution seems to be that adopted by a good number of commercial publishers. A 'book-processing charge' will be payable by either a research funder or institution, this covering peer review, editing, design and layout, hosting on the publisher's website, and possibly more. Indexing will still remain the responsibility of the author it appears. Design templates may be used to reduce costs, this being particularly appropriate for book and monograph series.

---

[38] https://creativecommons.org/share-your-work/cclicenses/   .

[39] https://www.ukri.org/publications/ukri-open-access-policy/uk-research-and-innovation-open-access-policy/#section-requirements-for-long-form-publications

[40] https://www.doabooks.org/en/researchers

[41] https://archive.org/about/

[42] OA book business models https://oad.simmons.edu/oadwiki/OA_book_business_models

One of the criticisms of this model has been that in developing countries, research funding often does not include publication funding of any kind, so the author may have to provide this personally. It is reported that some young academics fall for the costs of vanity publishers, so it may not be entirely a question of not being able to pay the book-processing charge. It is quite noticeable that Africa and the Middle East have very low percentages of research publications available via OA, but the reasons for this seem unclear. An upcoming conference in South Africa on this in early 2024 may address this issue, and more OA issues.

So, should an author pursue the OA route? It really comes down to exposure versus royalties. The royalties on academic publications are very small, as noted above. There is no difference in the processes pursued by good publishers in acceptance of OA manuscripts. So the fact that your book is available through OA has no effect on its credibility. The other major factor is speed. OA books, and particularly monographs, are often produced in under three months. Certainly, this is thus a viable route for academic authors to pursue.

Chapter 10.
THE EDITORIAL DEPARTMENT

Finally, after all the work of writing, presenting the manuscript in an acceptable form, and contract terms agreed, the goal is in sight, at least for the author. One of the first questions any author wants to know the answer to is, 'When?'. The answer of three, six, nine months, or a year, or even more is given, always produces a sigh of disappointment. Very very occasionally books have been published in weeks.

> A famous case is of the world's fastest-ever published paperback (at that time). It resulted from an important international gathering in the seventies, was a tremendous feat – three weeks or so – before computers. What was not so impressive were the vast number of errors that made the book almost unreadable: an embarrassment to all the writers involved and the publisher. Would you want that in your book? Assuredly not.

Having said that, many publishers including Palgrave and W.W. Norton, have adopted faster to publication models, notably for monographs, especially for OA, as noted above. This has come from intense pressures from academics and others, firstly in the sciences but now universally, who want to see research available for other academics to build on and utilise. As noted above, a major report was released in 2017, at The Academic Book of the Future,[43] and a Palgrave Pivot book[44] produced. One of the many outcomes has been the adoption of the far-faster publication of monographs, led by the Palgrave Pivot series. Three months or less are possible, as noted above.

So, let me look at the numerous processes that the publisher goes through to make the book as good as possible, bearing in mind all the other constraints. It is worth detailing here how the author interacts with these processes.

Let's now assume your manuscript has been presented perfectly, or that you have been through the peer review and/or developmental editing processes, and the manuscript has now been accepted. The publisher's acquisitions editor will put the book 'into production'. This may go through a 'production editor' who oversees all the work from copy editing to print or

---

[43] https://academicbookfuture.org/

[44] https://link.springer.com/book/10.1057/9781137595775

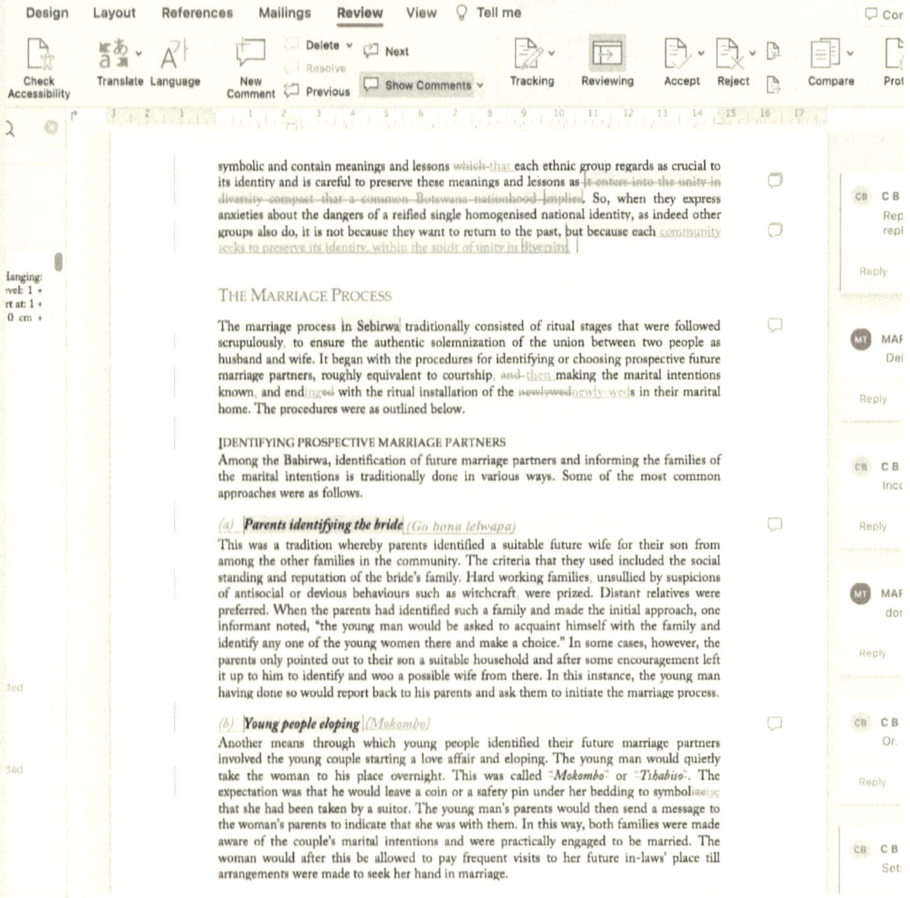

An example of an edited galley proof in **MS Word 2021**

symbolic and contain meanings and lessons ~~which~~ that each ethnic group regards as crucial to its identity and is careful to preserve these meanings and lessons as ~~it enters into the unity in diversity compact that a common Botswana nationhood implies~~. So, when they express anxieties about the dangers of a reified single homogenised national identity, as indeed other groups also do, it is not because they want to return to the past, but because each community seeks to preserve its identity, within the spirit of unity in diversity.

THE MARRIAGE PROCESS

The marriage process in Sebirwa traditionally consisted of ritual stages that were followed scrupulously, to ensure the authentic solemnization of the union between two people as husband and wife. It began with the procedures for identifying or choosing prospective future marriage partners, roughly equivalent to courtship, ~~and~~ then making the marital intentions known, and end~~ing~~ed with the ritual installation of the ~~newlywed~~newly-weds in their marital home. The procedures were as outlined below.

IDENTIFYING PROSPECTIVE MARRIAGE PARTNERS

Among the Babirwa, identification of future marriage partners and informing the families of the marital intentions is traditionally done in various ways. Some of the most common approaches were as follows.

(a) ***Parents identifying the bride*** *(Go bona lelwapa)*

This was a tradition whereby parents identified a suitable future wife for their son from among the other families in the community. The criteria that they used included the social standing and reputation of the bride's family. Hard working families, unsullied by suspicions of antisocial or devious behaviours such as witchcraft, were prized. Distant relatives were preferred. When the parents had identified such a family and made the initial approach, one informant noted, "the young man would be asked to acquaint himself with the family and identify any one of the young women there and make a choice." In some cases, however, the parents only pointed out to their son a suitable household and after some encouragement left it up to him to identify and woo a possible wife from there. In this instance, the young man having done so would report back to his parents and ask them to initiate the marriage process.

(b) ***Young people eloping*** *(Mokombo)*

Another means through which young people identified their future marriage partners involved the young couple starting a love affair and eloping. The young man would quietly take the woman to his place overnight. This was called "*Mokombo*" or "*Tshabiso*". The expectation was that he would leave a coin or a safety pin under her bedding to symbol~~ize~~ise that she had been taken by a suitor. The young man's parents would then send a message to the woman's parents to indicate that she was with them. In this way, both families were made aware of the couple's marital intentions and were practically engaged to be married. The woman would after this be allowed to pay frequent visits to her future in-laws' place till arrangements were made to seek her hand in marriage.

ebook production. A publishing plan will be made and a schedule and final costs will be worked out. Decisions on layout, type, artwork, photographs, typesetter, designer, artist and desk editor (in-house or freelance) will be made. This will be a quiet period for the author, but there will be plenty going on. A publisher's team coordination plan needs to be agreed, as will how the book fits into the rest of the publishing programme, from editorial, marketing and sales perspectives. Authors need a good deal of patience at this stage.

To start the production process, the desk editor, or copy editor, receives the manuscript with instructions from the acquisitions editor or even the publisher.[45] Copy editing is a fine skill, and it often surprises

---

[45] The head of a publishing company is usually called the publisher in smaller specialist publishing enterprises. There may be several publishers in larger companies.

authors just how many 'red marks' go into their manuscripts. The editor may not be a specialist in the author's area. This may prove advantageous to the author, as queries from the non-specialist will hold much validity – as a potential reader of the book. However, the editor chosen will have a keen interest in the subject matter. She or he will be able to raise pertinent questions where an explanation is not clear, or where vocabulary is used that may not be widely enough understood.

Some publishers prefer to typeset and format the author's final manuscript before copy editing. This can make the manuscript easier to edit, since paragraph styles will have been applied throughout. Indeed, the overlap of job functions has led to the typesetter and editor being the same person. The author will first then be sent galley proofs (see below) rather than corrected manuscript, and this speeds up the production process.

Standardising specialist spelling is a key function of an editor. The author may be consulted on preferences where conflicts appear, but with technical vocabulary it is very much up to the author to ensure correctness. Editorial work is also done using software, as well as by eye, so universal changes may be made quickly and easily. The editor, and the author at proof stage, should simply mark as 'change throughout' any word or phrase that needs that, rather than flogging through every case of its occurrence, and probably missing some.

A major cause of serious delay at the editorial stage is content querying. If the editor finds sentences that are unclear, the queries will be referred to the author, and it is most important that the queries are answered rapidly, within days, not weeks. Unanswered or late-answered content queries can cause an editor to move to another manuscript, and so compounding the lost time, and risk reducing the editor's interest. The editor, faced with too many unanswered content queries – which should have been sorted out earlier, will have less time for refining the language of the manuscript.

A note on production schedules

You should receive a draft schedule as soon as your book goes into production, which involves you at most stages. It means all the work leading up to the final ready-to-print (or making an ebook) pages. The schedule will involve a fair number of people and so needs adhering to by everyone, once agreed. For you, this means responding to editorial queries and returning proofs in good time. Of course, everyone involved is human, however much we use machines, even AI. So everything that can go wrong will go wrong, Mr Murphy was dead right on that, and publishing production seems to like gremlins.

> **Tip:** So, any time you cannot meet a deadline, be sure to let your editor know immediately so that the schedule can be revised.

Many a publisher will use project management tools, Gantt charts particularly, that will show a timeline, often with parallel activities, people involved and costs.

Early in my publishing career, I was handling a textbook series that went through trialling in three countries, and was published over seven years. The hand-drawn paper Gantt charts filled my walls! Now a big screen and software does the same, faster and, perhaps, better.

Proofs

The 'perfect first edition': a big prize offered! That would be quite an offer, but would the prize ever be won? A perfect first edition is what we are all after, prize or not: no spelling errors, no grammatical errors, no punctuation errors, no formatting or printing errors, and so on.

Bessie Head, my friend and perhaps Africa's most famous and accomplished woman writer, for many years never accepted any editor's changes to her manuscripts, saying that she had punctuated that way for a reason, used those words for a purpose. It used to give her editor quite a headache I was told, and at least one of her books does indeed make difficult reading. The occasional literary genius can do that, but most authors do find the input of editors highly invaluable.

Do remember that your editor is on your side, and acting in your best interests. They will not be making corrections and suggestions just for the sake of them. Do bear in mind their expertise or interest in your subject area, and acting as an informed reader of your published book.

So, to ensure an error-free book, there are a set of procedures that are followed, and these involve proofs at several production stages. Typesetting and copy editing may often be combined in a single process, so, as noted above, it is very possible that the first thing an author will see is a galley proof, the formatted edited text only. The author will be asked to respond to editorial queries, and to check and approve the final text content of the book. The publisher will expect the author to check the galleys religiously, and answer all queries in full.

At about the same time as a galley proof, the author will also be sent remade and resized diagrams, charts and any other illustration for content checking. Tables may also be included as separate items. Publishers' practices vary somewhat.

Layout: print and ebooks

Printed works and ebooks go through the same layout processes, but the layouts will be different in most cases.

Print book layout starts with a 'master page', which determines the page size and margins, and includes headers and footers. There will be several master pages, probably a different one for each chapter. With printed books, derived from pdfs,, the page design is fixed. With ebooks, however, the text is resizable and so the illustrations will not necessarily have the same positioning as in the printed version. Some, such as online 'flipbooks', use the pdf format perfectly though. It is also possible to have ebooks derived completely from pdfs on most distribution platforms, the only drawback being that they are hard to read on phones as there is no text flow. The advantage of putting up a pdf through an ebook platform is security from piracy.

For a print version, you will most probably receive a pdf as a page proof, and unless you have pdf-editing software, you will have to send your corrections manually in a separate document, referring to page and line numbers. Ebook page proofing practices vary widely between publishers, but the key points made about editing and galley proofs above still apply.

Why errors happen: last-minute changes

Following the return of the galley proofs the page layout and design will be completed, incorporating all the text and illustrations, including tables and graphs. There should be no changes to any material at this stage, and a publisher may insist on the author paying the cost of remaking pages if the changes are the author's. Changing pages is time-consuming and can have a knock-on effect throughout the whole book, from the positioning of illustrations to captions, page numbering, table and diagram cross-referencing, contents and index lists, sometimes completely remaking index page numbers. So, with all these factors, it's easy to see why errors can creep in. Additionally, there is at least one or less stage of proofing available for the changed bits, possibly producing error creep. The British Publishers Association actually published, many years ago, a small booklet titled something like 'Page Proof Changes Cost Money', very out of date, but still relevant.

So, the strong message is, do not make changes to page proofs unless really necessary. Do make sure that all corrections, additions or deletions are made to galley proofs, or be humbled. As E.A. Bucchianeri puts it, 'One piece of wisdom a writer quickly learns – typos keep you humble'.

Extra proofs

If only one set of proofs is produced, there is a higher risk of error. Rather, many publishers would rather produce further galley or page proofs if there have been extensive changes or corrections. But this comes at a cost, both financially and in terms of time. So, if the changes or corrections are author-based, the publisher may well expect the author to carry such additional cost.

Index completion

Once a final page proof is produced the page numbers can be inserted in your index if you are producing it. This needs to be done extremely rapidly, often within a week, so make sure you will have the time set aside. You can still add or delete entries. A professional indexer, if you or your publisher has employed one, needs to have advance notice of the page proof coming, to fit into their schedule, so make sure that you keep in touch on this.

Covers and back cover blurb (or back matter)

Your ideas for a cover will have been solicited at an early stage, possibly on the author information form. The cover is a key marketing tool, so decisions on this will be in the hands of your publisher, probably contractually so. I have always found that there is little disagreement after a bit of toing and froing.

The other key element is the back cover, often omitted in ebooks (regrettably: it can just follow the cover page in that case). This is a sales pitch, and quickly summarises the book, with information on what a wonderful author you are of course. You may have pre-publication review extracts also. In the first place, I always ask the author to do a first draft. I then turn it into easy-to-visually scan attractive text.

Multi-author works: differences

The number of authors of multi-author works may range from two to a conference proceedings with dozens of authors. Such works may also include multi-disciplinary chapters. It is good to bear in mind that the readers will also be from different areas of specialisation and, thus, fewer areas of knowledge may be assumed. A good guide is that, if your editor does not understand a term, it may not be suitable for many of the readers.

Scheduling of multi-author works is often more critical since more people are involved. Keep up to date with your editor on when proofs can be expected, as all those involved will need to keep time free. The book will not proceed to the next stage unless all proofs are back. The general editor will, on occasions, need to be really hard-headed to get proofs back from contributors. It is sometimes necessary to drop papers completely if certain critical queries cannot be answered. Failure to meet deadlines also causes contributions to be dropped from a volume.

Usually, only galley proofs are sent to individual authors and contributors. And sometimes not even those. All the proofing may be left in the hands of the general editor, or those of a small editorial committee. In whichever case, it is important that only one person has direct dealings with the publisher or publisher's editor, at least for most communications.

The general editor will need to get permission and copyright clearance for reproduction from individual contributors. This may be in terms of a full publishing contract, but more often a simple waiver or assignment form will suffice: the publisher can help the general editor to devise this, or provide a standard one.

Dissertations and theses

Dissertations and theses are rarely published by a commercial publisher in their original form. To produce a book or monograph, they may instead be expanded or reduced from the originals. Research results should be produced in summary table form, as a book will not usually contain original raw research data, notably that of a statistical nature. It may well be necessary to have an expanded introduction so that the research is placed in context, something that the thesis itself may have been able to assume since the readership was very specific. The findings might have to be restated to fit the understanding of a less-specialised reader. A good article is here: Revising the Dissertation into a Monograph,[46] and a quick search will find many more.

A PhD thesis can be the source of more than one publication, possibly several monographs and journal articles. There are opportunities here, not to be missed. Speak to your supervisor and colleagues. The same processes above still need to be gone through, and all the caveats I have talked about with about self-publishing and vanity publishers need to be looked at carefully. A good example of an Australian institution tackling the problem of predatory publishers is here.[47]

[46] https://www.palgrave.com/gp/book-authors/your-career/early-career-researcher-hub/revising-the-dissertation

[47] https://www.library.sydney.edu.au/research/strategic-publishing/?section=predatory-publishers

Chapter 11.
SALES AND MARKETING

The selling and marketing of books is one of the major functions of a publisher. But even with high print run 'trade' books and popular fiction, an author has a role to play in terms of publicity. Hence book launches at booksellers, or on line. For the academic writer, there is also a sales and marketing role.

The publisher should have a publicity form for an author to complete (see example page overleaf). The author will have more information to hand about journal publications and people in the specialist author's field than anyone in a book publishing house. Journals, reviewers, conference dates, TV and radio programmes, podcast interviews, and main and subsidiary market information will be immediately available to the author. The same goes for providing e-mail addresses.

An author who collects some copies en route to sell at every conference will get a smile from the publisher. Prior to publication, the author can also hand out fliers that the publisher will send to authors, also for emailing. Friends, colleagues and others in your address book, receiving an email from you as the author, are far more likely open these than one from a publisher's mailing.

And then there's Facebook, LinkedIn, X (exTwitter) and any other social media platform you have a decent following on. These can only serve you well. Importantly, in your posts make sure you put a picture of your cover, or you holding your book. Your 'friends' on social media will probably include people you don't even know.

Reviews are a wonderful marketing tool. Encourage readers of your book to post them on Amazon.[48] Goodreads is also an excellent source of reviews. Both of these are only possible post-publication however.

Your book should be on Amazon, at least as a print edition, but perhaps as a Kindle ebook too. If not, ask your publisher to get it there quickly. Check that the cover, ISBN and book description are correct.

As well as your book launch and those mentioned above, your personal and institutional websites, Ted Talks, and becoming a guest on a podcast are all valuable sources of publicity. For the self-publisher 70+ Book Mar-

---

[48] Only those who have spent at least £40 on Amazon UK, $50 on Amazon US, in the last 12 months may do so there.

keting Ideas to Rocket-Boost Your Sales[49] gives a good idea of the immense amount of work needed, and the cost.

AN EXAMPLE OF PART OF AN AUTHOR'S PUBLICITY FORM

PROMOTION

1. Please list, in order of importance, all institutions, professional organisations, government departments, companies, NGOs, etc., to which your book would be of interest. Please give contact name, e-mail address, telephone and WhatsApp numbers wherever possible.

2. Do you or any of your contacts have access to any lists of postal or e-mail addresses to which publicity material could usefully be sent? YES/NO. If YES please specify owners of lists.

3. Where else should we send promotional literature? Can you suggest any other suitable mailing lists, either postal or e-mail? From where can we acquire them? Please give full contact details.

4. Do you know of any forthcoming conferences or professional meetings where participants would be interested in your book or it might be displayed? YES/NO. If you are attending, can you distribute publicity material? YES/NO/NA. How many copies would you like? •   Can you obtain a mailing list of participants/can we insert material in mailings by the conference organisers? YES/NO/NA. Please provide the name of the conference, its dates and venue, and the organiser's name and full contact details.

5. Are there any well-known people who, because they know you or because of their special interest in the subject, might be willing to provide an endorsement or favourable advance opinion about your book if they were sent a proof copy? Would they allow us to quote them? YES/NO Please indicate if you have already approached them in this respect.

6. Promotional material for your own use: please indicate the number of copies of any promotional material that we produce that you can distribute via friends, colleagues, etc.

REVIEWS and PUBLICITY

1. Please indicate names of professional and other journals which you believe are very likely to carry a review of your book. Please list in order of importance.

Newspapers/Magazines/Specialist Journals/Overseas Journals.

Please list under these headings:

(a) Botswana

(b) UK

(b) USA

(c) African Countries

---

  https://blog.reedsy.com/book-marketing-ideas/

Chapter 12.
STAYING IN PRINT, NEW EDITIONS, AND GOING OUT OF PRINT

The hardest thing for a publisher to maintain in print is slow-selling but valuable academic work. Even straight reprints may be delayed as demand may be slow to absorb the reprinted copies. It may, in particular, be difficult to go to a second edition since the first edition printing may well have mostly filled the market. The publisher may well consider going for only ebook or print-on-demand sales. They will find it far easier to keep the book in print if these routes were used in the first place, and this is happening increasingly.

The complexities of costing and forecasting reprints and new editions can be frustrating for both author and publisher. Eventually, the only way to keep a title literally 'in print' may be only an e-book, either for sale, or free through OA.

A publisher will almost certainly have the capacity to sell over the web, so if your book is contractually 'out of print' and not intending to reprint, you are within your rights to take the book to another online ebook or print publisher, or self-publish it. A common contractual provision is for the author to give six months' notice to the publisher of intent to request reversion of the copyright. Once the book is no longer available, your contract should have a clause in it stating how long it will be until the reproduction rights revert to you, or whoever is the copyright holder.

The further option of reprinting using 'print on demand',[50] digital printing, may sometimes prove viable, even if expensive as even only single copies are printed, to order. You will see this on Amazon where there is a long delivery time for an order. The higher price demanded by the higher print costs may put your book out of the market, however.

You may be told by the publisher that the level of stock of printed copies held is low, or sometimes you may notice in a royalty statement. Do then discuss the above options with your publisher. This would, naturally, not apply in the case of already print-on-demand books or ebooks,

---

[50] For initial low print runs, certainly under 200, and possibly as high as 500, may be printed in this way. This may help to explain the high prices being charged for academic books with small print runs.

by their very nature. But decisions can be difficult, so exercise some patience on this one: a good month's wait.

A last option is when a printed book is 'remaindered'. This will occur if your book is not selling and simply taking up warehouse space. It means that remaining copies of your book can be sold off for whatever the publisher can get for it, possibly to booksellers who may offer the remaindered copies off cheaply, possibly to institutions. Your contract should have a clause in it about this, especially regarding royalties, and you should have the option to purchase at the remaindered net price.

Finally, what happens to the publisher's digital files? And in what software will they be? And will the publisher be prepared to hand these files over? It is unlikely that any contract has clauses that cover these questions. If you have retained your original manuscript, that will help, but even better would be if you received galley proofs in digital form. You could also scan your book to digitise it to pdf, and then convert it to Word. There is software that you can use for this, even by uploading to dedicated websites.

And here are two sites you might find useful: Rights Reversion[51] and Re-Publishing an Out-of-Print Book After a Rights Reversion[52]

---

[51] https://www.authorsalliance.org/resources/rights-reversion-portal/

[52] https://www.authorimprints.com/re-publishing-out-of-print-book-after-rights-reversion/

Chapter 13.
THE END (OF THE) MATTER?

If you like this book, do write a brief review, on Amazon, or anywhere
that you bought this book from.

****

Do you need more help with your book?

Or need to publish?

Or just get editing, formatting, and layout done?

And then get your book distributed?

****

Or want to give me criticism or suggestions?

I am only too happy to respond to your queries,
and help guide you at:
publisher@lightbooks.co.bw *and*
lightbooksbotswana@gmail.com

****

And do visit

…my company website, www.lightbooks.co.bw

…my personal one www.charlesbewlay.com, and

…Linked In: Search for Charles Bewlay

Chapter 14.
FURTHER READING

Bloomsbury Academic (2024) *Writers' & Artists' Yearbook 2023.* Bloomsbury Yearbooks 117th edition. London. 816pp

Germano, William (2016) *Getting It Published: A Guide for Scholars and Anyone Serious about Serious Books.* Third Edition, University of Chicago Press, Chicago and London. 304pp.

Luey, Beth (2009) *Handbook for Academic Authors 5th Edition.* Cambridge University Press, Cambridge. 296pp.

Portwood-Stacer, Laura (2021) *The Book Proposal Book: A Guide for Scholarly Authors (Skills for Scholars),* Princeton University Press. Princeton and Woodstock, 216pp. There are also some excellent articles on this book, including excerpts, at How to impress an acquisitions editor[53] *and* The Peer Review Process: What Sets University Presses Apart[54] *and* Trying to get your scholarly book published?[55]

Rabiner, Susan & Alfred Fortunato (2002) *Thinking Like Your Editor How to Write Great Serious Nonfiction -- and Get It Published.* W.W. Norton, United States. 288pp.

---

[53] https://www.universityaffairs.ca/career-advice/ask-dr-editor/how-to-impress-an-acquisitions-editor/

[54] https://janefriedman.com/the-peer-review-process-what-sets-university-presses-apart/

[55] https://press.princeton.edu/ideas/trying-to-get-your-scholarly-book-published-some-tips-for-maintaining-perspective-and-staying

Appendix.
THE BOOK PRODUCTION PROCESS

Below is a summary of the stages that a manuscript goes through to produce a book. It is in rough time sequence, although there will often be overlap, particularly in matters relating to covers, indexes and marketing. Publishers vary in their processes, but what is presented here should give a broad, and I think representative, picture for the author.

Manuscript assessment: readers
Marketing consultation
Distribution consultation
Costing and viability

Editorial/author info form
Letter of intent to author/customer
Contract issuance

Content/developmental editing,
Copy editing (possibly after galley proofs)
Edited manuscript or galley proof checking (editor & author)
Hyperlinks checking
Type design

Layout mock-up
Cover ideas – discuss with author/artist/designer
Illustrator briefs

Typesetting and formatting
Galley proofs
Proof checking (editor & author)
Galley proof correction

Layout
Design finalisation

Publicity form
Cover brief

Page makeup
Graphics, illustrations & tables into pages layout
Page proofs
Page proof checking (editor & author)
Page proof to indexer

Cover roughs
Page proof correction
Index & tables of contents etc. updates
Cover finalisation

Convert files to pdf

Check printer's proof
Plates production
Printing
Binding

Packing
Delivery/collection
Distribution

THE PUBLISHER'S MARKETING AND SALESPEOPLE WILL HAVE BEEN BRIEFED ON THE PROJECT FROM THE START, AND HAVE A PARALLEL PROGRAMME. THAT WOULD BE THE SUBJECT OF A DIFFERENT MONOGRAPH THOUGH.

Acknowledgements

I could not have made this book possible without the unbridled criticism, help and encouragement of Michael Britton,[56] Lisel Erasmus-Kritzinger,[57] Frank Youngman,[58] Jim McCall,[59] Neil Parsons[60] and Fred Morton.[61] They saw the manuscript in the order of the stage at which they received and critiqued it. So Michael and Li received the most raw version, and opened my eyes to seeing just how raw it was. Frank knocked me over with later suggestions, and Neil threw more of the writer's light on the manuscript. Jim gave an enlightened publisher's perspective, while Fred added some serious writer's finesse.

All come from professional writing, including academic, editing and publishing. They make me realise the great friends I have from the wonderful worlds. of writing, editing and publishing. And jazz in some cases. A great big thank you to everyone.

Any remaining errors are of course mine, no doubt caused by my last minute changes to page proofs.

---

[56] https://michaelbritton.co.za/bookcase/

[57] https://www.gettextbooks.co.uk/author/Lisel_Erasmus-Kritzinger

[58] https://www.researchgate.net/profile/Frank-Youngman-2

[59] https://www.linkedin.com/in/jim-mccall-b4124b1a/?originalSubdomain=uk

[60] https://neilparsons.me/history-biography-1

[61] https://ub-bw.academia.edu/FredMorton

About the Author

Charles has spent his life in publishing since 1981. His first ten years in educational publishing with Macmillan gave him a broad grounding in the field. There he ran a seven-year tri-national mathematics project, and also commissioned hundreds of titles in the sciences, social sciences and humanities. After ten years he started his own niche publishing company, focusing on academic and  research publications, women's NGO works, and a miscellany of occasionally interesting books such as a tertiary-level law textbook and a secondary school computer science introductory coursebook. He has also been commissioned as a production consultant by top research institutions in Botswana, including a SADC/EU evaluation project under the Botswana Institute for Development Analysis, the regional Institute of Development Management, University of Botswana faculties, the Bank of Botswana (the state bank), and the Vision 2016 and 2036 organisations.

Charles has been deeply involved in every aspect of book publishing throughout his career. He has taken on every aspect of it, being in the frontline of editing, proofreading, commissioning, designing and laying out books, marketing, and project management. He is continuously learning, taking on new directions, sometimes stumbling and falling; investigating the depths, but never drowning. Now, here is his 'inside story' to guide you. What he writes is based on his experience, but he does draw on the wisdom of others, gained over many years.

Before publishing he was a highly dedicated mathematics teacher, the best in the world, or so he says. Charles loved teaching, but he left it because of an opportunity to join publishing, and ended up loving that too.

Charles went to 12 schools in seven countries, his first memory being of how to write 2345, and not 2000345, at the age of four. In his final school year he received the top prize for mathematics. At university in the UK, his study of mathematics and physics was sidelined by much zeitgeist and his interests in philosophy, politics, economics, art and photography, which became paramount. He became, and remains, both a polymath and an autodidact. During his postgraduate training as a further education lecturer he was able to focus on the effects of language, particularly African ones, on schoolbook publications.

His great loves, outside publishing, writing and mathematics, are music, literature, history, fine art, and photography,[62] but firstly his wonderful family and friends.

P.S. My last words from my original published chapter, on which this little book is based.

"Well, my journey of living an author's life is over for a bit. I am behind schedule, not at all happy with what I have written, and hoping the editor will give me some flak and hard criticism. The exercise has given me more admiration for the so many authors who have become good friends over the years, and I hope that through the above I will have created more friendships for others in these two most rewarding of lives, writing and publishing."

---

[62] https://charles856.wixsite.com/bewlayphotography

INDEX

www.ingramcontent.com/pod-product-compliance
Lightning Source LLC
Chambersburg PA
CBHW021343160726
47994CB00007B/2830